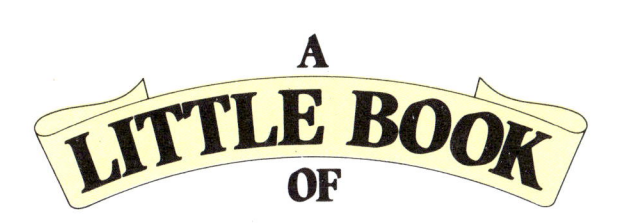

A LITTLE BOOK OF Rainbow stories

ILLUSTRATED BY
Ivan Ripley

HUTCHINSON
LONDON · MELBOURNE · AUCKLAND · JOHANNESBURG

Produced by Templar Publishing Ltd,
107 High Street, Dorking, Surrey RH4 1QA,
for Hutchinson Children's Books

This edition copyright © Templar Publishing 1987
Illustrations copyright © Templar Publishing 1987

All rights reserved. No part of this publication may be reproduced, stored in a retrieval system, or transmitted in any form or by any means, electronic, mechanical, photocopying, recording or otherwise, without the prior permission of the publishers and the copyright owners.

First published 1987 by Hutchinson Children's Books
An imprint of Century Hutchinson Ltd,
Brookmount House, 62-65 Chandos Place, Covent Garden,
London WC2N 4NW

Century Hutchinson Group (Australia) Pty Ltd,
16-22 Church Street, Hawthorn, Melbourne, Victoria 3122

Century Hutchinson Group (NZ) Ltd,
32-34 View Road, PO Box 40-086, Glenfield, Auckland 10

Century Hutchinson Group (SA) Pty Ltd,
PO Box 337, Bergvlei 2012, South Africa

Set in Times Roman by Templar Type

British Library Cataloging in Publication Data

A Little book of rainbow stories.
   I. Ripley, Ivan
   823'.01'089282 [J]   PZ7

ISBN 0-09-171800-7

Colour separations by Positive Colour Ltd, Maldon, Essex
Printed and bound by L.E.G.O., Vincenza, Italy

Contents

· 4 ·

The Red Teapot

· 9 ·

Carrot and the Orange Wig

· 14 ·

The King who loved Yellow

· 18 ·

The Green Umbrella

· 23 ·

Boy Blue

· 28 ·

Rainbow's End

The Red Teapot

by Gina Stewart

The red teapot sat miserably on the shelf in the dark cupboard where it had been put months ago. It had been sitting in the same place for so long it had grown dusty and had lost all its shine. To make matters worse, a spider had woven its web around the handle, something the red teapot found very ticklish and uncomfortable.

At least today the cupboard door was open, and the teapot could see what was going on. There seemed to be a lot of activity in the kitchen, with people coming and going and packing everything in sight into large boxes.

"Careful with that china!" said Mrs Morris, the owner of the red teapot. "I don't want it broken before it gets to the new house!"

"So that's what all this is about!" thought the red teapot. "We're moving to a new house!"

And for a while, the red teapot felt happier, hoping that in the new house it would be cleaned and polished and loved.

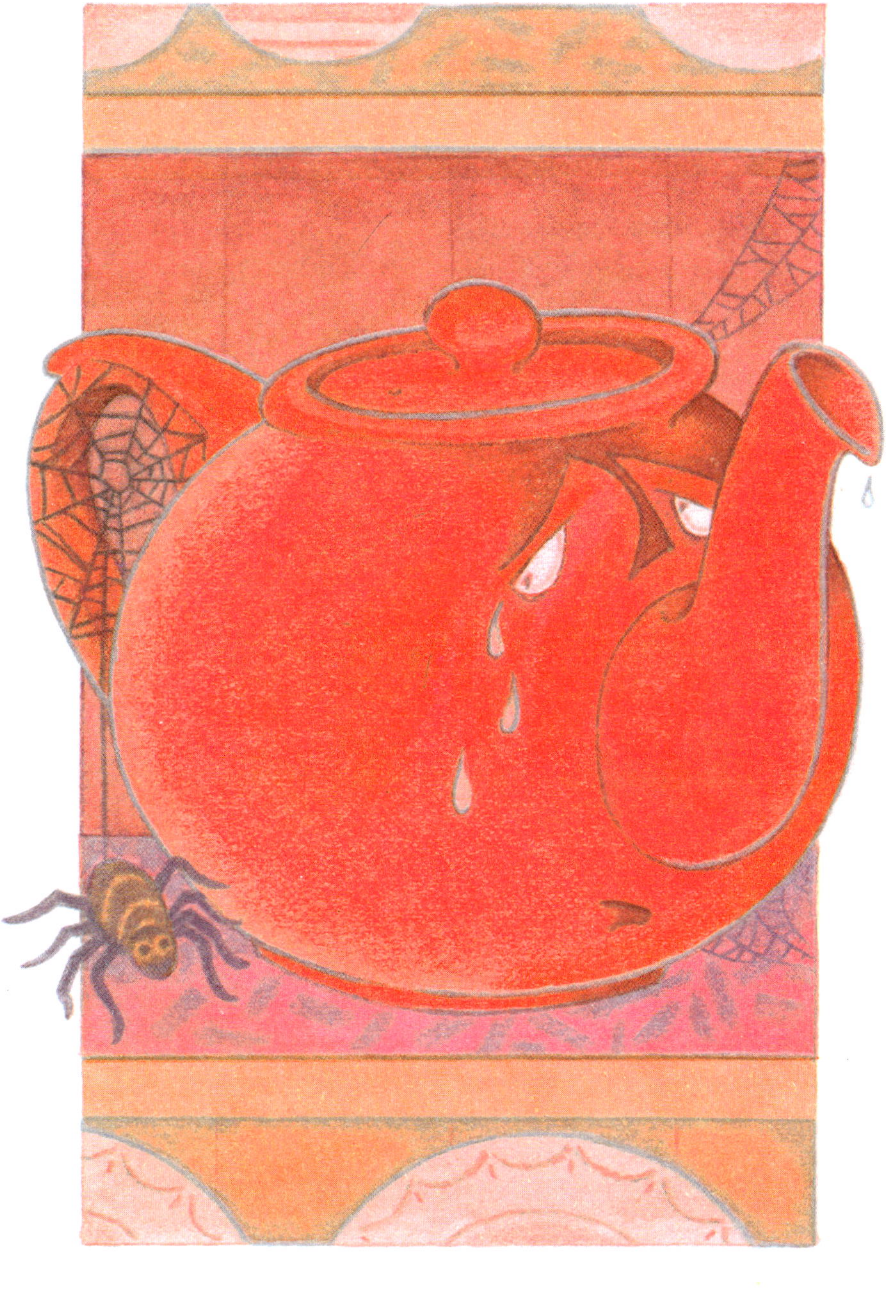

From the dresser, Mrs Morris took down a white teapot with gold leaves painted on it and a gold rim around the lid. It had a fine, elegant handle and a long, narrow spout.

"This is my best teapot," she told the removal men. "I think I'd better pack it myself."

"It's no use," thought the red teapot sadly. "I could never sit next to something like that. I'm much too plain and fat."

Just then one of the removal men opened the cupboard door.

"What about the stuff in here, Missis?" he asked Mrs Morris.

The red teapot was very pleased. Now at last it would be brought out of the dark cupboard and have its cobwebs washed away.

Mrs Morris took a quick look inside the cupboard.

"Just pack up those glasses," she said. "The rest is only rubbish. It can stay where it is."

And so the red teapot was left in the dark cupboard, with nothing but a couple of plastic mugs for company, while the glasses and the white-and-gold tea-set and all the rest of the crockery and cutlery went with Mrs Morris to her new house.

That night the red teapot felt very lonely and sad. Even the spider had left the teapot handle and gone to spin a new web in another part of the cupboard.

Next day, the red teapot was woken up by a new sound: it was the noise of children laughing and running about.

"Look what's in here!" shouted a small boy, flinging open the cupboard door.

"It's a teapot!" said his sister, carefully taking the lonely red teapot down from the shelf.

"Let me see!" said a second girl, who was rather bigger than the first. Very carefully, she wiped away some of the dust. "Isn't that wonderful" she said. "It's a red one! It'll go perfectly with our red-and-white striped mugs and plates!" Just then, their mother walked into the kitchen.

"Look, Mummy" said the children. "We've found a red teapot!"

"Well, fancy that!" said the children's mother and she carefully washed and dried the red teapot until it shone and sparkled. "It isn't even chipped!" she added, cheerfully. "Why, this is just what I've been looking for. A nice, round, sturdy teapot to use every day!"

And with that, she put the red teapot right in the middle of the sideboard so that everyone who came to the house could see it.

"I think we're going to like our new home, don't you?" said the children's mother.

"Yes!" they all shouted.

"And I think I'm going to like *my* new home, too!" thought the red teapot happily.

Carrot and the Orange Wig

by Sally Sheringham

Carrot the Clown was feeling down in the dumps. For some time now Mr Whipp, the ring master, had been hinting that Carrot's act was not popular enough, and that he might have to replace Carrot with a younger, funnier clown. And now something dreadful had happened – Nancy, the circus goat, had eaten Carrot's orange wig.

"I'm so sorry, Carrot. I must be getting short-sighted," she bleated, almost in tears herself. "I thought it was spaghetti in tomato sauce, and you know how I eat anything that doesn't move. If it's any help, it tasted horrible."

As far as Carrot was concerned, that was no help at all.

Mr Whipp wasn't at all sympathetic. "What's the good of a clown without an orange wig?" he roared, so angrily that his top hat trembled. "I can't have a bald clown! If you don't find yourself a new orange wig straight away you'll have to go, Carrot. And that's final."

So Carrot ran down to the wig maker's shop.

"I'm afraid we don't have much demand for orange wigs, Sir," said the wig maker politely. "But I think you'll find this black one suits you very well."

Carrot explained that only orange would do. "That's why I'm called Carrot, you see," he said. "If I had a black wig I would have to be called something like 'Coal' or 'Night', and I'm far too old to change my name. I suppose I'll just have to give up being a clown," he added, and a large tear trickled down his white cheek.

Carrot went off to the park. He sat down on a bench, put his head in his hands, and thought hard about his future. The circus was his whole life. What could he do if he had to leave it?

Suddenly he heard the sound of a throat being cleared. He looked up. It was a cat, with fur so orange that it made Carrot blink. The cat asked him what the matter was, and Carrot told her the whole, sad story. The cat, whose name was Marmalade, then told Carrot her own unhappy story. She had been turned out of her barn by the farmer for not catching enough mice. "But I don't want to waste my life catching mice," sighed Marmalade. "I want to be famous, and you don't become famous hidden away in a barn."

Carrot and Marmalade sat silently for a moment, trying to think of some solution. Suddenly they both shouted, "I've got it!"

"Are you thinking what I'm thinking?" said Carrot. Marmalade nodded, excitedly. It was a brilliant idea that should solve everything!

When they explained their plan to Mr Whipp his eyes nearly popped out of his head. "You're both quite mad," he declared. "It'll never work. And that's final!" But eventually they persuaded him to let them try it once.

It was a great success! The audience roared and roared with laughter. They had never seen a clown with bright orange hair that wriggled and purred, and knocked off his bowler hat and waved goodbye at the end of the act. They would certainly be coming back to see Carrot and Marmalade again – and again!

Even Mr Whipp found it funny. "I have to admit that you two make a great double act," he laughed, drying his eyes. "You can both stay at the circus for as long as you want. And that's final!"

Carrot and Marmalade danced for joy.

"I accept, on condition that I don't end up where Carrot's first wig did," joked Marmalade, winking at Nancy Goat.

"Don't worry, I only eat things that don't move," said Nancy, eyeing Mr Whipp's top hat.

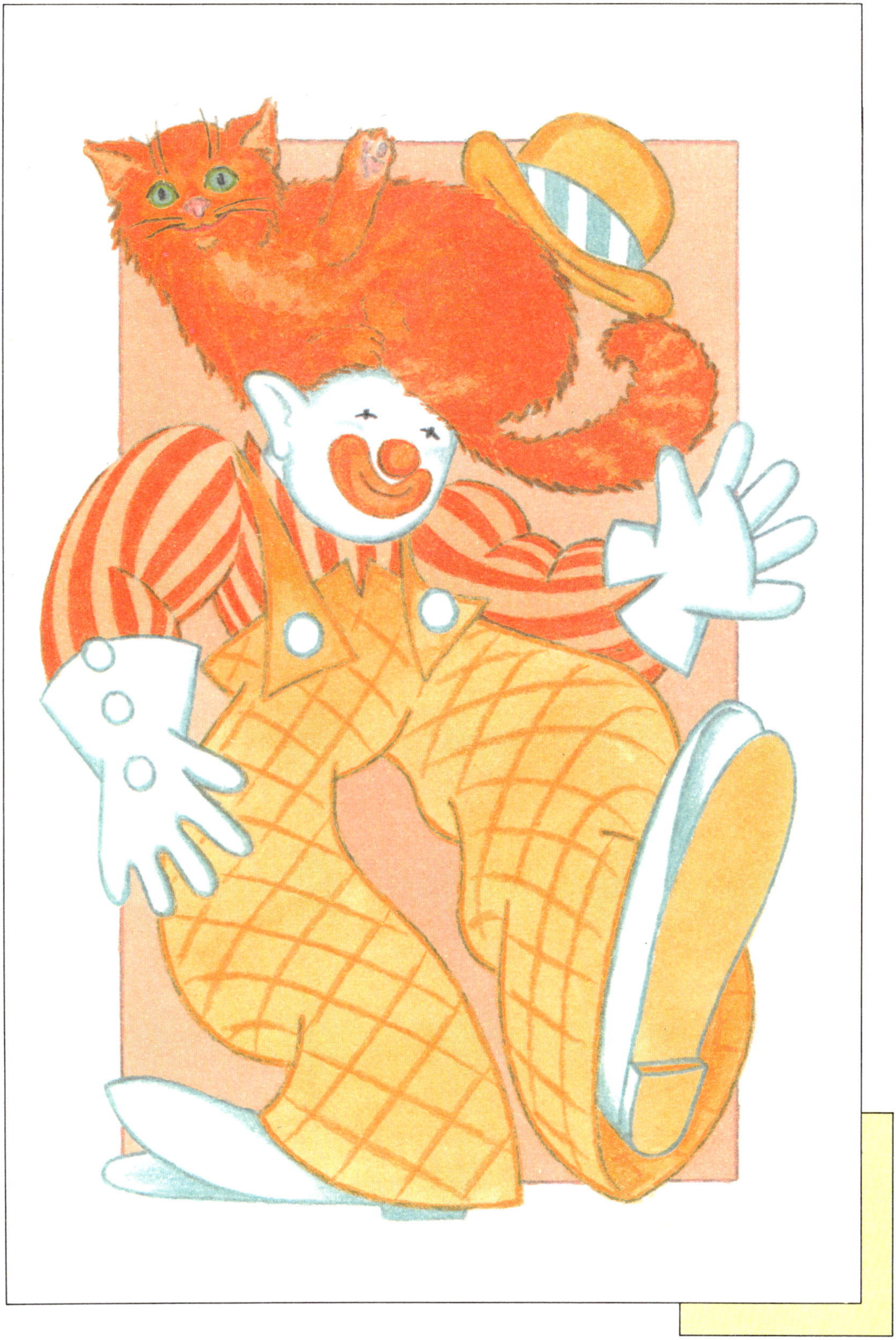

The King Who Loved Yellow

by Philip Steele

There was once a king called Colin the Great whose favourite colour was yellow. He wore yellow robes and a yellow crown, and lived in a yellow palace. His throne room was filled with canary birds in yellow cages and his breakfast was served on yellow dishes.

Now Colin had everything in the world that a king could possibly want. He had a golden coach, precious jewels and hundreds of servants to wait on him.

The neighbouring kingdom was very different. Its ruler was a cousin of Colin. His name was Peter the Poor and he ruled a very poor kingdom. Peter's palace was only a small one, and its roof let in the rain. He had sold his crown years ago, to pay the rent. Why, he had only one horse to ride about his kingdom! But it *was* a very special horse – it was yellow! When Colin heard that his cousin had a yellow horse, he was mad with jealousy.

"Just think of it!" he said to the queen. "A yellow horse! Can you imagine me riding it at the head of the big parade? It would match the flags and uniforms! It would be perfect! Such a horse is wasted on a fool like Peter! *I* want it! I *deserve* it!"

That very evening King Colin put on a false beard and moustache and rode away to the kingdom of Peter the Poor. By dawn he was at Peter's palace. He sneaked in to the stables. There it was! A beautiful yellow horse with a mane of pure gold. Colin quickly swapped his own horse for Peter's, and galloped off as fast as he could.

King Peter was furious.

"That scoundrel has everything he wants!" he shouted. "I have nothing! Yet he robs me!"

King Peter decided to see if his grandmother could help. She was a wise old woman, who lived in a ruined tower on the border between the two lands. Her name was Kitty and some people said she was a witch. When he told her what had happened, Kitty looked at him with a twinkle in her eye.

"Now's the time to teach that silly ass a lesson," she said. "Just leave things to me…"

The next morning will never be forgotten in the kingdom of Colin the Great. It started raining custard! Great dollops of yellow pudding dribbled down the window panes of the palace. When King Colin went to the bathroom, steaming custard came gushing from the taps! Colin saddled his yellow horse and rode to the seashore. Great yellow waves were crashing on the beach!

Colin hurried back to the palace, wiping custard from his hat.

"I've had enough!" he stormed. "I never want to see yellow again! And take this nasty yellow horse back to my horrid cousin! It's Kitty who's behind this!"

Well, the horse was sent back, and the spell came to an end. And from that day onwards no one in King Colin's land was allowed to wear yellow clothes, or eat yellow sweets, or grow yellow flowers. But do you know what everyone called him behind his back? His Royal Highness King Custard the Great!

The Green Umbrella

by Stanley Bates

Upstairs on the double-decker bus sat the green umbrella, next to her owner. She was trying to look out of the window, but she wasn't quite tall enough. The bus stopped, and some people got off. When the green umbrella looked around, she saw that she was all alone – no one was sitting next to her!

"Wait for me!" she shouted. "Don't leave me behind!" But it was too late. The bus had started to move off again. The green umbrella tried very hard not to cry. "Oh dear," she said. "I've never been out on my own before."

After a while the bus conductor came upstairs and, as he leant across the seat to wind up the window, he noticed the green umbrella huddled in the corner of the seat.

"Hello, someone's left their umbrella behind again. They never forget them when it's raining," he said, as he picked it up. "A very nice green one!" And he took it downstairs and put it into a small cupboard under the stairs. "I'll hand it in to the Lost Property Office when we get back to the depot," he said to himself.

The cupboard was very small and dark. The green umbrella was very frightened, but soon fell asleep. When she woke up, the bus had stopped. The cupboard door opened, and the conductor took the umbrella out. Then he walked over to a door marked 'Lost Property'.

"Here you are, Bert. Another lost umbrella for the collection."

"Thanks," said the man in charge of Lost Property. "It looks brand new – shame someone lost it. You don't see many green umbrellas."

Then he put a label around the green umbrella's handle, with a number on it, and put it on a shelf with lots and lots of other umbrellas.

The green umbrella had never seen so many umbrellas before. There were even more here than in the shop where she came from. Old black umbrellas, grey umbrellas, stripy umbrellas, broken umbrellas – but only one green umbrella.

"Ca-can you tell me where I am, please," said the green umbrella, in a quiet voice.

A large black umbrella, with a silver band on his handle, said in a loud, deep voice, "We're in the Lost Property room at the bus station."

"Yes, I know that," said the green umbrella. "But I would like to go home now."

Nobody said anything, so the green umbrella said again, "I would like to go home *now*."

All the other umbrellas started whispering together.

"You tell her."

"No, you tell her," they were saying.

"I'll tell her," said a Scottish tartan umbrella from the other side of the room. "You see, m'dear," he explained kindly, "we've all been forgotten, so I'm afraid that there's not much chance of ever going home again."

"That's right!" squeaked a small stripy umbrella. "I've been here for weeks, waiting to go home."

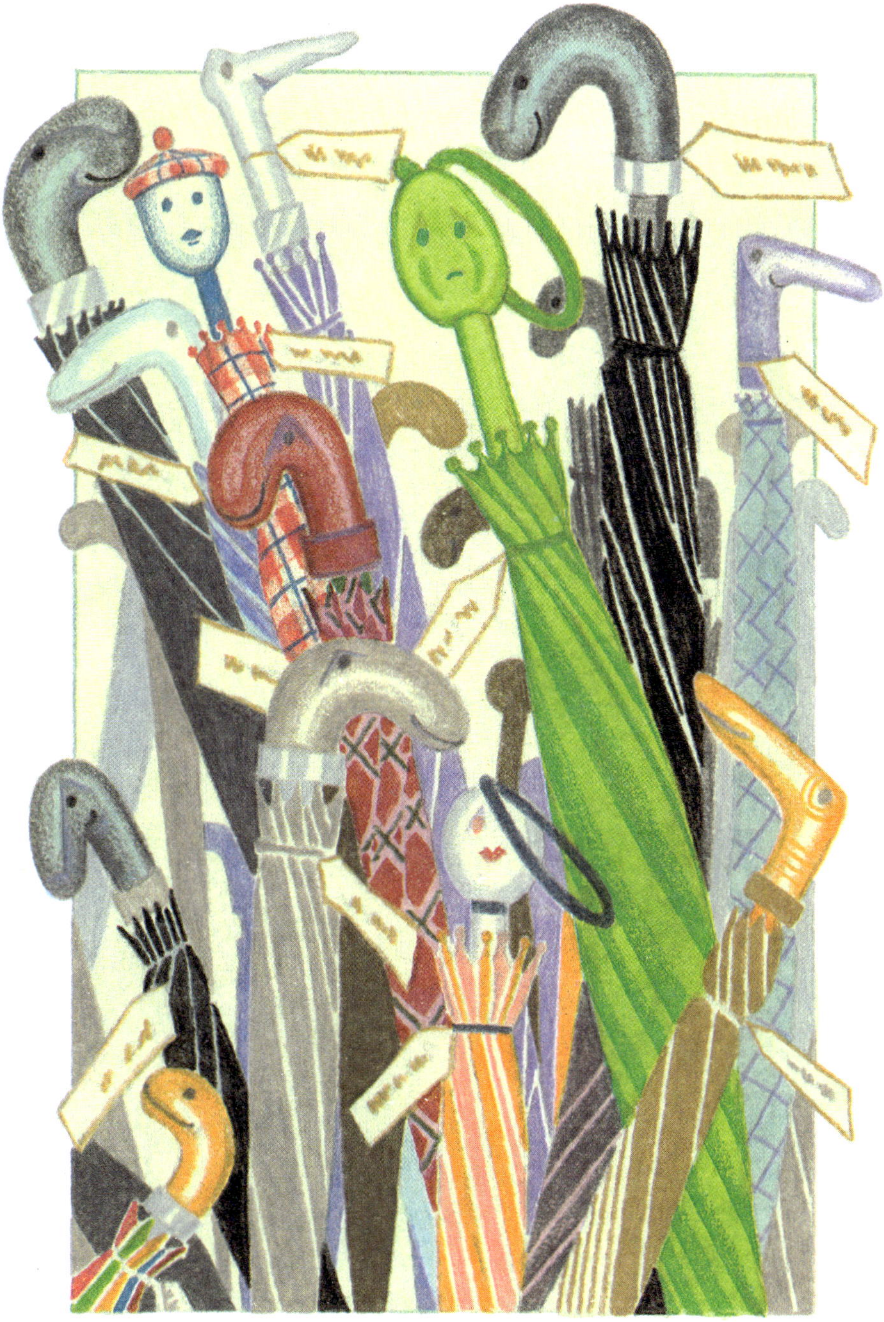

"Don't worry, though," said the tartan umbrella. "We're all friends here, so try to make yourself at home."

As the days went by, the green umbrella settled down with all the other umbrellas. She was very happy with her new friends, but never forgot about her real home. Then, one day, she heard the Lost Property man talking to someone.

"… A green umbrella? Hm! Let me see. I do seem to remember one."

"Yes!" shouted the green umbrella in her loudest voice. "It's me! I'm over here!"

"Ah, yes!" said the man. He gently lifted the green umbrella off the shelf, and handed her back to her owner, who was thrilled.

"Yes, yes, that's the one. Oh, thank you so much! I thought I'd lost it for ever!"

So the green umbrella said goodbye to all her friends, and went back home with her owner. And although she had enjoyed meeting all those other lost umbrellas, she was very, very glad that, unlike them, she hadn't been forgotten after all.

Boy Blue

by Jane Varley

Blue was a doll. He lived with Sara and went everywhere that Sara went. When Sara went to the supermarket with her mum, Blue went too. Sometimes he rode in the seat of the shopping trolley. Sometimes Sara wanted to ride in the trolley too, but she couldn't any more because her legs had grown too long. Sara was five.

Sara loved Blue very much and gave him a special place to sit on the shelf in her bedroom. At night Blue slept under Sara's pillow.

Blue was a rag doll and everything about him was blue. Not just his eyes and his clothes. No, Blue had blue legs, blue arms, a blue face and blue hair. Even his tummy was blue under his blue shirt. But Blue hadn't always been blue, and he hadn't always been called Blue, either. When he first came to live with Sara he was like any other rag doll and Sara called him 'Boy'. "That's not a name!" said Sara's mum. But Sara liked it. Boy had pale yellow hair made of wool and a sweet pink face. His arms and legs were pink, and he wore a white shirt and blue trousers.

One bright, sunny morning Sara's mum came into her bedroom early.

"Up you get Sara-Sue," she said. "I have exciting plans for today."

Sara rubbed her eyes, fished Boy out from under her pillow and shuffled into the bathroom. Mum had run a bath and the room was filled with steam. Now, whenever Sara had a bath, Boy was allowed to come too, but he had to sit on the shelf above the laundry basket, because rag dolls can't have baths. They get all soggy and squidgy.

"Today," said Sara's mum, as she rubbed Sara all over with a soapy sponge, "today we make a start on your bedroom. I think it looks dull and drab. How about a nice new colour scheme? Don't you think blue would be nice?

I can't buy anything new, so I thought we could dye your curtains and quilt cover to match the paint. We'll go to the launderette and use the big washing machines there to do the dyeing."

As soon as they'd eaten breakfast, Sara and her mum gathered up the curtains and the quilt cover and stuffed them into a big dustbin sack.

"Can I have blue sheets and pillow cases too?" asked Sara.

"Well, why not," said her mum. "I'll just get the dirty ones from the laundry basket."

Soon Sara and her mum were on the bus on their way to the launderette. Suddenly Sara let out a wail.

"Mum! I've forgotten Boy. Where is he?"

"I haven't seen him today, but I'm sure we'll find him when we get home," said Sara's mum, and gave her a cuddle. But Sara was upset. Boy was always getting lost. Suppose he had hidden himself again? And suppose this time she couldn't find him?

When the dyeing was finished, Sara and her mum caught the bus home again. Sara's mum went out to hang the blue things up to dry.

"What's this lump in your quilt cover, Sara-Sue?" asked Sara's mum.

She reached inside the wet cover and fished out a very soggy and completely blue lump.

"Oh Sara, love," cried mum. "It's poor old Boy. He's gone all blue!"

Sara said nothing. She took Boy from her mum and looked hard at him.

"You're a naughty boy to hide away," said Sara. "But I love you anyway. And I like blue just as much as I like pink and yellow."

"I think I'd better hang him up to dry," said Mum, and she pegged Boy to the line.

"When he's dry, he'll match my new room," said Sara, with a giggle. "And I can call him Boy Blue. Blue for short."

So Blue got his proper name and a new colour. He went everywhere with Sara but he never tried hiding again – except, sometimes, in the blue bedroom.

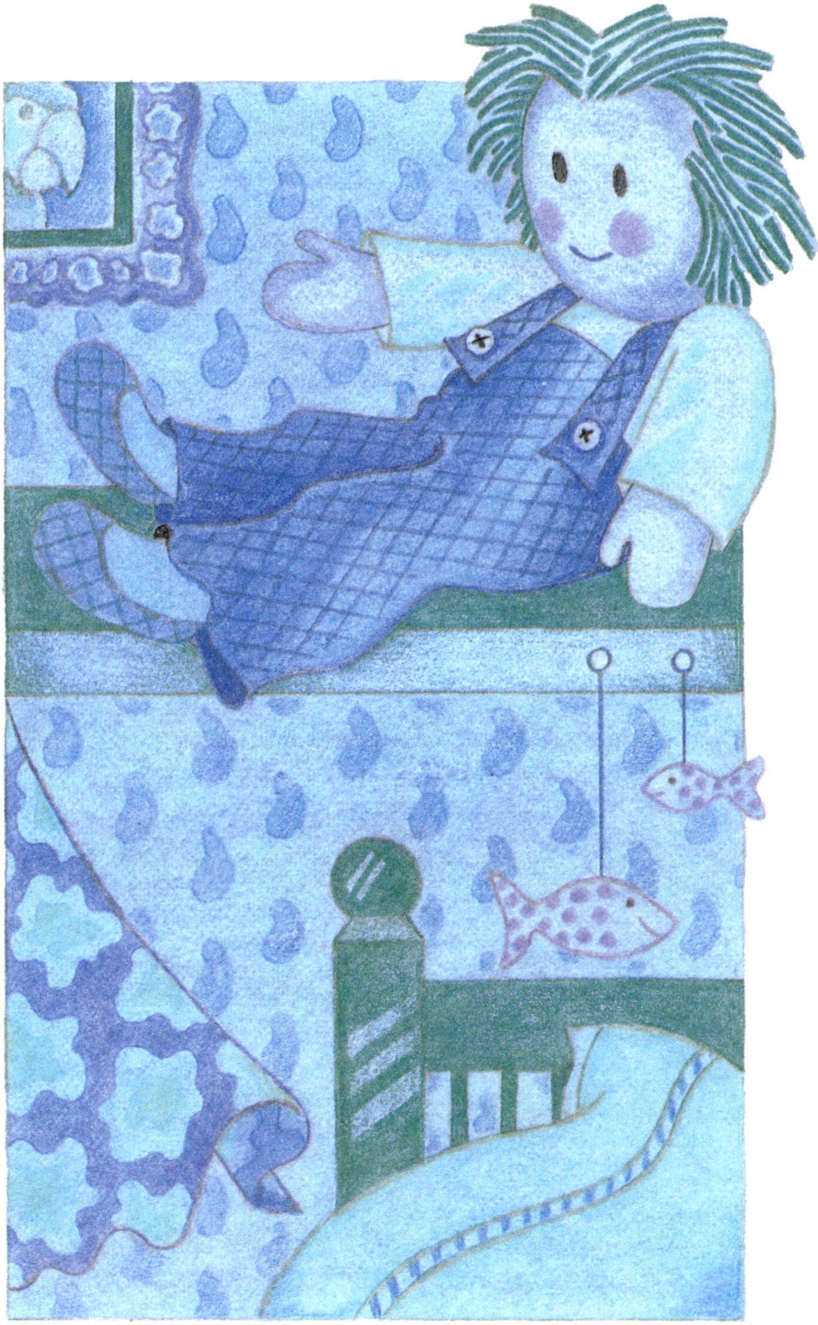

Rainbow's End

by Philip Steele

This is the story of the rainbow's end, and a puffin who got in a pickle. The puffin's name was Percy, and he lived far away in the green, salty seas of the West. He was a dumpy little bird with a round, white tummy and a sleek, black back. His feet were bright orange and webbed, and he had a beady eye.

All in all, Percy looked very comical – but he was not a happy puffin. For a start, it was a lonely life at sea. And when Percy did meet other birds, they always laughed at his beak. It was a corker! It looked as if it had been designed to crack walnuts instead of catch fish.

"*Parrot face!*" the gulls used to scream at him.

Percy had another complaint – the weather. If you have ever heard the forecast for shipping on the radio, you will know what it's like out there on the western seas. It gales and hails, it sleets in sheets, it blows and snows and rains in torrents.

One morning in early spring, Percy sat on his rock. He had a beak full of fish, but his feet were freezing! A pale sun was shining, but it was raining, too. Just *his* luck!

Percy gulped down his fish – and then nearly choked with amazement! Stretching over the sea was the most beautiful thing he had ever seen in his life. It arched right into the sky in a shimmer of light. It was red and orange and yellow, like the dawn. It was green and blue and indigo, like the sea. It was a hazy violet colour, like the sea pinks that grow in the cliffs. Beneath the arc in the sky, the sea was silvery-grey, and a little fishing boat was trawling to and fro. Percy could hear the fishermen's voices carrying across the water.

"That's a fine rainbow, to be sure," said one.

"Do you know what my old granny used to say?" replied the other. "At the end of every

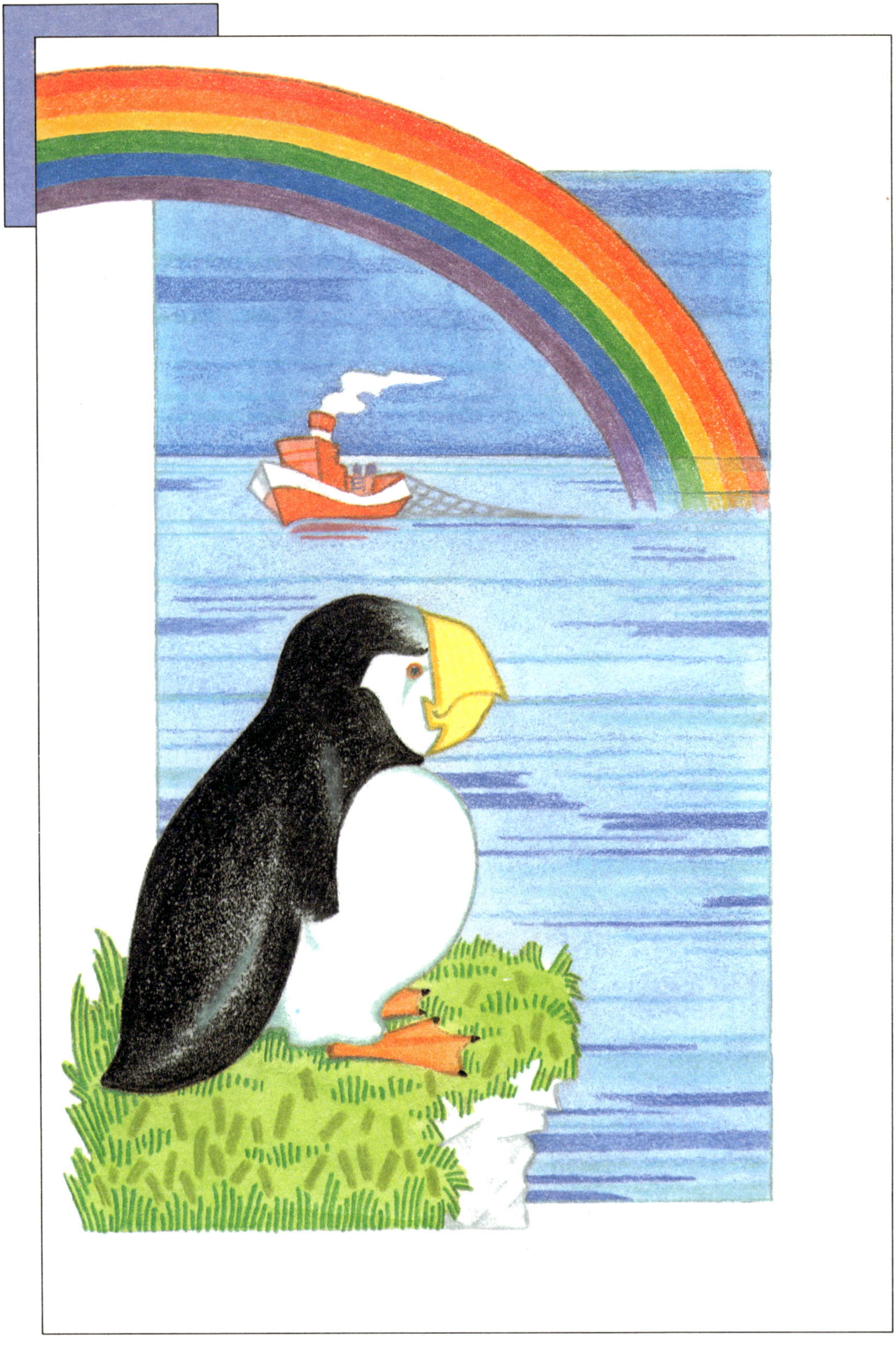

rainbow there's a crock of gold, and all your wishes come true!"

So this was a rainbow! Percy was excited. Just suppose – if he could find its end, all his wishes would come true! Why, he could have all the fish he could eat, and a nice dry clifftop burrow to live in, *and* a beak like – like a seagull! There and then Percy the Puffin made a decision. He would fly to the rainbow's end.

Percy spread his wings and skimmed over the waves. He flew for miles. The wind blew up and the rain came down, but on he flew.

"Percy perseveres," he squawked, which was his way of saying "I shall carry on and on". And so he did. Or at least he tried. The trouble was, the rainbow seemed to stay just ahead of him all the time. He could not catch up with it, let alone find out where it ended. His wingbeats were getting weaker, until at last he could carry on no more. He fluttered down to the sea.

The fine rain eased off and disappeared. And as it did so, the magical rainbow faded. Percy dipped his beak beneath the waves, as if to say goodbye. The sun dipped below the horizon. Percy felt very sad. He would never find the rainbow's end, and never see his wishes come true.

The next day Percy was cross with himself. Chasing rainbows indeed! Whatever next! He slowly flew back to his rock.

The gulls looked very surprised when they saw Percy. And to his amazement, they didn't make fun of him at all.

"I think your beak looks very *smart*," said one gull.

"I wish I had a beak like *yours*," said another.

Puzzled, Percy waddled over to a rock pool and looked down into it. There, in the still water, he could see his reflection. His beak was still a funny shape – but it was coloured like a rainbow!

Then he remembered that he had dipped his beak into the sea as the rainbow faded. Perhaps some kind of magic had been at work ... rainbow magic!

Percy was a proud puffin. And even though he hadn't been to the rainbow's end, he lived happily ever after.

But that's not the end of the magic. It's still going on today. Every spring, the puffins head home from the wintry oceans. And every spring, their dark, drab beaks take on stripes of brilliant colours. Perhaps it's in memory of Percy, who tried to find the rainbow's end.